QUILTING
with Anne Orr

by Anne Orr

DOVER PUBLICATIONS, INC.
New York

Copyright © 1990 by Dover Publications, Inc.
All rights reserved under Pan American and International Copyright Conventions.

Published in Canada by General Publishing Company, Ltd., 30 Lesmill Road, Don Mills, Toronto, Ontario.
Published in the United Kingdom by Constable and Company, Ltd., 3 The Lanchesters, 162–164 Fulham Palace Road, London W6 9ER.

Quilting With Anne Orr, first published by Dover Publications, Inc., in 1990, includes instructions for all of the quilts shown in *Anne Orr Quilts: Pattern Book*, published by Anne Orr Studios, Nashville, Tennessee, in 1944. Several photographs originally in color are reproduced here in black and white and one photograph has been omitted. Five pattern pieces have been redrawn and three new diagrams have been added. The text has been revised to reflect modern materials and techniques.

Manufactured in the United States of America
Dover Publications, Inc., 31 East 2nd Street, Mineola, N.Y. 11501

Library of Congress Cataloging-in-Publication Data

Orr, Anne Champe.
    Quilting with Anne Orr / by Anne Orr.
        p.   cm.
    Rev. ed. of: Anne Orr quilts. 1944.
    ISBN 0-486-26325-8
    1. Quilting—Patterns. 2. Patchwork—Patterns. I. Orr, Anne Champe. Anne Orr quilts. II. Title.
TT835.O77 1990
746.9'7—dc20
                                           90-21569
                                             CIP

Preface to the Dover Edition

Anne Orr, needlework editor of *Good Housekeeping* magazine for 21 years, was one of the most influential needlework designers of the first half of the twentieth century. In addition to her magazine work, she produced scores of needlework books that are still collected today by those who love good design.

Although she was best known for her charted designs, Anne Orr designed for all needlework techniques—knitting, crocheting, tatting, embroidery and, of course, quilting. It is with great pleasure that we present this volume of her quilt designs.

The quilts shown here include both patchwork and appliqué. In several of the quilts, Ms. Orr combined her expertise in the medium of charted design with the technique of patchwork to create stunning pictorial quilts. Other quilts feature appliquéd jonquils, garlands or strawberries.

Materials and techniques have changed since this book was originally published in 1944. For example, no longer is 36" the standard width for fabrics sold over the counter. We have therefore revised the text to reflect such changes. The quilts themselves, however, are just as Anne Orr first presented them.

General Instructions

Materials

The best fabrics for quilting are light- to medium-weight 100% cottons. If you must use a blend, pick one with no more than 30% synthetic fiber.

Wash all fabrics before cutting them to check that they are colorfast and preshrunk. Do not use fabrics that continue to bleed after they have been washed.

Press the fabric to remove wrinkles and crease marks. Check the grain line of the fabric carefully. Lengthwise threads should be parallel to the selvage and crosswise threads should be perpendicular to insure that the pieces will be correctly cut. If the fabric is off-grain, pull it gently on the bias in the opposite direction to the off-grain edge to straighten it.

All fabric requirements are based on using 44"–45" wide fabrics. If your fabric is narrower, you will require more.

Patterns and Templates

All of the patterns given in this book are actual-size and are printed on one side of the paper only.

Two types of patterns are given—template pieces, which include a seam allowance, and cutting or placement guides.

To use the templates, remove them from the book and glue them to lightweight cardboard. Carefully cut them out along the solid cutting line. If you do not want to destroy the pages of the book, trace the templates and glue the tracing to cardboard. For more permanent templates, trace the patterns onto translucent plastic. Place the templates on the right side of the fabric and trace around them with a sharp pencil. Whenever possible, pieces with straight edges should be placed next to one another so that they share a common cutting line.

Remove the required placement guide from the book or trace it onto tissue paper. Glue the guide to sturdy cardboard to make it last longer. Place the guide underneath the fabric; you should be able to see the design lines clearly. If not, use a light table or hold the fabric against a sunny window. Trace the design. Dressmaker's tracing paper can also be used to transfer the pattern; in this case, make several tracings of the pattern and do not glue them to cardboard.

Trace the cutting guides to the fabric in the same way, or if you wish, you can make cardboard templates for them.

Patchwork

All patchwork pieces are sewn with the right sides together, using a ¼" seam allowance. The seams can be sewn by either hand or machine. After stitching, press the seams to one side, toward the darker fabric if possible. On pieces with a large number of patches, try to press the seams in alternate directions—i.e., press all of the seams in one row to the right, those on the next row to the left.

When you complete a block or section of patchwork, you should block it before joining it to another section. Pin the piece to an ironing board or other padded surface, making sure that all of the corners are perfectly square. Using a steam iron or a dry iron and a damp cloth, press the edges first, then the center. The piece should be perfectly flat with no puckers.

Appliqué

Before beginning, trace the placement pattern to the fabric. Pin the appliqué pieces to the fabric, following the placement guide. Attach the appliqués with a blindstitch, turning under the seam allowance with the point of your needle as you stitch. The seam allowance on most appliqué pieces is quite narrow—just over ⅛". Use thread to match the appliqué. The appliqué should just cover the guideline on the quilt and the stitches should be nearly invisible. If one piece is to be applied on top of another, attach the top piece first, then sew the lower piece to the quilt top.

If you are a beginner to appliqué, you might find it helpful to turn under and baste the seam allowance on each appliqué piece before pinning it to the quilt top.

Quilting Patterns

A quilt consists of three layers—the quilt top, the batting and a backing. These layers are held together with quilting stitches.

Your quilt can be quilted with a wide variety of designs. For appliqué, one of the most common types of quilting is outline quilting—quilting around each shape about ¼" away. Outline quilting is also used on patchwork quilts, with the quilting following the seams of the patches. Parallel diagonal lines or diamonds are also a common quilting pattern.

Large areas of background can be filled with fancier quilting patterns. Dover Publications has a number of books offering a wide selection of such quilting patterns.

Outline quilting and straight line quilting do not generally need to be marked on the quilt top; however, more elaborate designs should be marked before the quilt layers are assembled. Mark all lines on the right side of the fabric using a hard lead pencil, chalk or one of the special water-soluble marking pens. The lines should be just dark enough to see. The quilting will cover the lines and the marks will not be apparent when the quilt is completed.

Backing and Batting

Fabric for the backing should be soft and loosely woven so that the quilting needle can pass through easily. Your quilt is probably wider than most available fabric, so you will have to sew lengths together to make your quilt back. When joining fabric, do not have a seam going down the center. Instead, cut off the selvages and have a wide center strip with narrower strips at the sides.

There are a number of different kinds of batting on the market. Buy a medium-weight bonded polyester sheet batting for most quilts.

Cut the backing and batting approximately 2″ wider on all sides than the quilt top. Place the backing, wrong side up, on a flat surface. Place the batting on top of this, matching the outer edges. Smooth the batting out so there are no lumps. Now center the quilt top, right side up, on top of the batting. Pin the three layers together, then baste from the center out to the midpoint of the sides and to the corners. Add additional rows of basting if necessary to keep the layers from shifting.

Quilting the Top

The actual quilting stitch is a simple process, but it does take a little practice. The stitch is just a very simple running stitch, but working through three layers at once may be a bit difficult at first.

Use one of the short, fine needles especially designed for quilting (they are called "betweens") and a 100% cotton quilting thread.

Wear a thimble on the middle finger of your right hand (or your left, if you are left-handed) to push the needle through the fabric.

The quilting can be done in a traditional floor frame or in a hoop. Whichever you use, the quilt should be held firmly with no wrinkles in the quilt top or in the backing. Begin working in the center of the quilt and work toward the outer edges. As you work, you will find that the quilting stitch has a tendency to push the batting, and by working from the center out you can gradually ease any excess fullness toward the edges. If you wish, run the quilting thread through beeswax to keep it from tangling.

Begin with an 18″ length of thread with a knot in one end. Go into the quilt through the top about ½″ from where you plan to begin quilting and bring the needle up on the quilting line. Pull gently, but firmly, and the knot will slip through the fabric into the batting, where it will disappear. Place the left hand under the quilt where the needle should come through. With the right hand push the needle vertically downward through the layers of the quilt until it touches the left hand, then bring the needle back to the top. As you become proficient at quilting, you will be able to do the whole operation with one hand, merely using the left hand to signal that the needle has penetrated three layers. Experienced quilters are able to put several stitches on the needle just as if they were sewing.

Make the stitches as close together as you can. The stitches should be evenly spaced, and the same length on the front as on the back. When the entire quilt has been quilted, lift it from the frame or hoop and remove the basting stitches.

Binding

If the edges of your quilt are straight, you can use either straight or bias binding. If the edges are curved, you must use bias binding.

For straight binding, cut 1¼″-wide strips across the full width of the fabric; join them to make a strip long enough to go around the quilt, plus about 2″.

For bias binding, fold the fabric so that the crosswise and lengthwise threads are parallel. This fold marks the bias. Mark diagonal lines parallel to the fold, 1¼″ apart. Cut on these lines and on the fold. Join the strips.

Trim the batting and backing even with the edges of the quilt top.

To attach either straight or bias binding, turn under ½″ on one end of the strip. With raw edges matching and right sides together, pin the strip around the quilt, mitering the corners. Overlap the ends. Stitch. Fold the binding to the wrong side of the quilt, turn in the raw edge and slipstitch it to the backing.

Notes on Working from Charts

On the inside covers of this book you will find color charts similar to those used in cross-stitch. Several of the quilts in the book are made using these charts. In addition, many other designs are included on the charts so that you can create your own quilts.

Each square on the color chart represents one square of fabric. These variously colored fabric squares are sewn together to form a design. The square can be any size, and patterns for different-size squares are given on page 28. Each instruction will indicate which pattern to use.

When making a quilt from a charted design, it is more practical to cut the pieces as you need them rather than to cut them all at once. Many of the designs require such a large number of patches that it would be impossible to keep track of them if they were cut at one time. Therefore, the instruction will not indicate how many squares of each color to cut, although in some cases you may be told how many to cut for a single block or unit of the quilt.

The square patches used for these designs lend themselves to quick cutting techniques. Cutting across the full width of the fabric, cut strips the height of the template. A rotary cutter can be used for this, and more than one layer of fabric can be cut at once. Cut the individual squares from these strips. Cut carefully to make sure the squares are the correct size.

Sew the squares together. For ease in handling, you can assemble the quilt in rows, or in blocks of ten squares in each direction as indicated by the heavy lines on the working diagram. Once the rows or blocks are assembled, sew them together, carefully matching the seamlines. Block the unit carefully to make sure that all corners are square.

Because of the large number of seams in many of these designs, it is possible that your patched piece will vary slightly from the dimensions given. Therefore, in cutting the borders and other pieces to be sewn to the patched piece, it is a good idea to cut them longer than required. The dimensions given in the individual instructions include this extra length. Once the border is sewn to the piece, trim off the excess, making sure that all edges are perfectly straight. When you are adding a large number of strips (as for the Oval Wreath or Heirloom Basket), be very careful to make sure the quilt does not become "lopsided."

Jonquil Quilt

Approximately 80″ × 104″

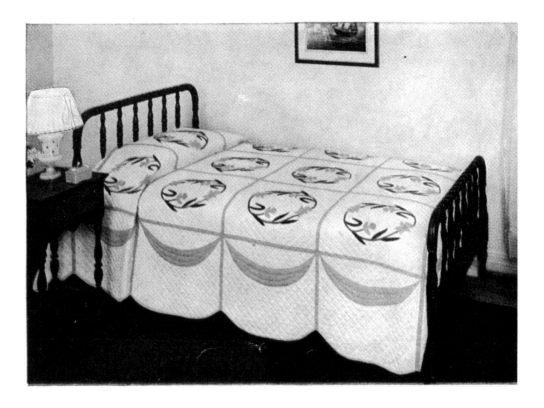

Fabrics

6¾ yds. white
3½ yds. light yellow
1 yd. green
¼ yd. dark yellow
6 yds. for backing

From white, cut 25 blocks 16½″ × 19½″ (place the 19½″ dimension along the crosswise grain of the fabric) and five partial blocks 9½″ × 16½″. From light yellow, cut eight side scallops, six end scallops and two loops. Cut 20 strips 1½″ wide across the full width of the fabric; join to make four strips 104″ long and four strips 80″ long. Cut appliqué pieces for twelve blocks; cut ½″-wide bias strips of green for stems. Each pattern piece is marked with the color and the number of pieces to cut for one block.

Mark the lengthwise and crosswise center of 12 of the blocks. Trace the placement guide to each of these blocks, matching the arrows to the folds. Rotate the guide 180° to trace the second half of the pattern. Pin the appliqué pieces in place, alternating the colors of the flowers and using dark yellow petals and insides with the light yellow cup and vice versa. Appliqué the pieces in place.

Sew three of the appliquéd blocks together along the long edges to form a row. Repeat with the remaining appliqué blocks. Sew the four rows together to form the center of the quilt.

Mark the crosswise center of four blocks. Pin a side scallop across each of these blocks matching the centers and having the points of the scallop just touching one long edge. Appliqué in place, leaving about 1″ at each point unsewn. Fold the points out of the way and sew the blocks together along the short edges. With the scallops on the edge closest to the center, sew the strip to one long side of the center of the quilt. Finish appliquéing the points. Repeat on the other side of the center.

Mark the crosswise center of three of the partial blocks. Pin an end scallop across the top of each and appliqué in place, leaving the ends unsewn. Sew the three appliquéd partial blocks together along the short edges; sew a plain partial block to each end. Sew this strip to the top edge of the quilt with the scallop against the center piece. Finish appliquéing the scallops.

Sew end scallops across three of the remaining blocks, leaving the ends free. Sew the blocks together; sew a plain block to each end of the strip. Pin a loop to each plain block, placing the narrow end in the upper inside corner. Appliqué, leaving the narrow end free. Sew the strip to the bottom of the quilt. Finish appliquéing the scallops and loops.

Assemble the quilt layers. Quilt around each appliqué piece. Quilt two lines through each scallop, following the curve. Quilt the remainder of the quilt in 1″ diamonds. Cut the edge of the quilt in shallow scallops following the shape of the appliquéd scallops. Pin yellow strips over the seams of the blocks and appliqué in place. Bind the edge of the quilt with light yellow bias binding.

The placement guide is on pages 16–17; the appliqué patterns are on pages 20–21.

Star Flower Quilt

See photograph on page 7
Approximately 98" × 117"

Fabrics

5½ yds. white
5 yds. blue
3 yds. pink
¼ yd. dark pink
½ yd. green
10 yds. for backing

Cutting along the lengthwise grain of the fabric, from white, cut two strips 1½" × 95" and two strips 1½" × 115" for the borders; cut thirty 11½" squares. From blue, cut eleven 3½"-wide strips across the full width of the fabric; join these strips to make two 97" and two 122" borders. Following the working diagram on the inside front cover and using patterns #1 and #2 on page 28, cut the patches for the design.

Sew the green and white triangles together to form squares. Piece together the flower that is in the center of each block. Make a total of 30 flowers. Fold each 11½" square in half lengthwise and crosswise to mark the center. Appliqué a flower in the center of each square. Following the working diagram and *Fig. 1*, sew the blue and pink star points around each square. Sew the squares together in six rows of five blocks each. Add one additional row of squares to the right-hand and top edges.

Sew the shorter white borders to the top and bottom of the quilt and the longer borders to the sides. Repeat with the blue borders.

Assemble the quilt layers. Follow the lines of the seams with the quilting, continuing the lines across the white squares. Bind the edges of the quilt with blue.

Fig. 1

Oval Wreath Quilt

See photograph on page 7
Approximately 74" × 99"

Fabrics

4½ yds. white
1 yd. very dark rose
¾ yd. each dark, medium and light rose
⅛ yd. each two shades of yellow, three shades of pink, two shades of blue and two shades of lavender
6 yds. for backing

Cutting along the lengthwise grain of the fabric, from white, cut two 12" × 90" strips, one 16½" × 34" strip, one 15" × 34" strip and one 6" × 34" strip. Cutting across the full width of the fabric, cut eight 2½"-wide strips from light rose, seven 3"-wide strips from medium rose, seven 3½"-wide strips from dark rose, and seven 4"-wide strips from very dark rose. Join the strips to make two 56" and two 90" light rose borders; one 60" and two 94" medium rose borders; one 65" and two 96" dark rose borders; and one 78" and two 104" very dark rose borders. Using pattern #4 on page 28 and following the working diagram on the inside front cover, cut the squares for the wreath and the pillow sham. Sew the squares together. Add three rows of white squares all around the wreath and the sham. Make sure that the wreath and the sham are the same width; adjust the seamlines if necessary.

Sew the 6"-wide white strip across the top of the sham and the 15"-wide strip across the bottom. Sew the wreath to the bottom of this piece, being very careful to keep the various pieces aligned. Sew the 16½"-wide strip across the bottom of the wreath. Sew a 12"-wide strip to each long edge of the piece.

Sew the short light rose borders to the top and bottom of the quilt, the longer borders to the sides. Sew the short medium rose border to the lower edge, the longer borders to the sides. Sew on the dark rose, then the very dark rose borders in the same way.

Assemble the quilt layers. Quilt a feather pattern around the wreath and the sham. Quilt the background in diagonal lines about 1" apart. Bind the top edge with light rose, the remaining edges with very dark rose.

Oval Wreath
Instructions on page 6

Debutante's Pride
Instructions on page 12

Heirloom Basket
Instructions on page 9

Star Flower
Instructions on page 6

An Initialed Quilt

Approximately 90″ × 104″

Fabrics

9 yds. off-white

3 yds. green

⅛ yd. each two shades of blue green, two shades of yellow green, three shades of rose, two shades of blue, two shades of yellow and two shades of lavender

8 yds. for backing

Cutting along the lengthwise grain of the fabric, from off-white, cut the center panel 32½″ × 100″; cut two strips 17½″ × 100″, two strips 7½″ × 100″ and four strips 1″ × 100″. Cut two strips 1″ × 108″ and two strips 1″ × 92″ for the borders. From green, cut two strips 1″ × 22″ and two strips 1″ × 28″ for the edges of the initial block. Cut two strips 1½″ × 100″, two strips 1¼″ × 100″ and four strips ¾″ × 100″. Cut two strips 1½″ × 108″, two strips 1½″ × 92″, two strips ¾″ × 108″ and two strips ¾″ × 92″ for the borders. Using pattern #3 on page 28 and following the working pattern on the inside back cover or below, cut the pieces for the desired initial and sew them together. Use two shades of yellow for the center of the white flower rather than the gray and yellow shown on the colored chart. Add enough off-white squares to each side to make the initial 40 squares wide. If you have to add an uneven number of rows, add the extra row on the right. Add 11 rows of off-white squares to the top and to the bottom of the letter.

Sew a 1″-wide green strip to the top and bottom of the initial block. Sew a 1″-wide green strip to each side. Press under the seam allowances on the edges of the block.

Center the initial on the center panel, having the top edge 44″ below the top of the panel. Blindstitch the block in place. Working out from the center, sew 100″-long strips to each side of the panel in the following order: ¾″-wide green, 1″-wide white, 1½″-wide green, 7½″-wide white, 1¼″-wide green, 1″-wide white, ¾″-wide green, 17½″-wide white.

For the borders, sew a ¾″-wide green strip to one edge of a matching 1″-wide white strip; sew a 1½″-wide green strip to the other side of the white strip. Make four striped borders. Pin the borders to the quilt edges with the ends extending evenly. Stitch, beginning and ending the stitching ¼″ from the corners. With the quilt top right side up, turn under the top border strip on each corner so that a 45° angle is formed from the inner corner of the border to the outer corner. Press the fold. Bring the edges of the quilt together with the right sides in and stitch the borders together, using the crease as a guide. Trim the excess.

Assemble the quilt layers. Quilt the center panel in diagonal lines 1″ apart, changing the direction of the lines at the center of the quilt. Continue these lines onto the wide off-white sections, changing the direction on each section. The initial block is quilted in diagonal lines through the center of each square. Bind the quilt with green.

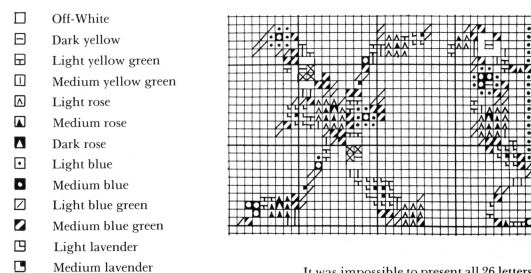

☐	Off-White
⊟	Dark yellow
⊞	Light yellow green
⊡	Medium yellow green
◪	Light rose
◭	Medium rose
◥	Dark rose
⊡	Light blue
◙	Medium blue
◿	Light blue green
◢	Medium blue green
⌐	Light lavender
◄	Medium lavender
⊠	Light yellow

It was impossible to present all 26 letters in full color, so the two least used are shown here in black and white.

Heirloom Basket Quilt

See photograph on page 7
Approximately 78″ × 96″

Fabrics

6½ yds. off-white
5 yds. medium blue
⅛ yd. each yellow, gray, light and dark blue, three shades of tan, three shades of rose and two shades of lavender
6 yds. for backing

Cutting along the lengthwise grain of the fabric, from off-white, cut two 16½″ × 80″ strips for the sides; cut a 9″ × 28″ rectangle, a 16½″ × 28″ rectangle and a 15½″ × 28″ rectangle. From blue, cut two strips 14½″ × 100″, one strip 14½″ × 60″ and one strip 7½″ × 28″. Following the working diagram on the inside front cover and using pattern #3 on page 28, cut the squares for the basket and the sham.

Sew the squares together. Add three rows of off-white squares around the basket. Add three rows of off-white squares to the top and bottom of the sham and five rows to each side. The basket and the sham should be the same width—about 24½″. If necessary, adjust the seamlines.

Sew the 9″-wide strip to the top of the sham and the 16½″-wide strip to the bottom. Sew the basket to the bottom of this piece. Be sure that all of the pieces are aligned properly. Sew the 15½″-wide strip to the

bottom of the basket. Sew the long off-white strips to the sides. Sew the narrow blue strip across the top of the quilt.

Mark the midpoint of the lower edge. Place the point cutting guide (page 28) along the lower edge, with the top point at the center and the lower edge on the raw edge of the quilt. Trace the point to the quilt; trace two points on either side of the center point, spacing them an equal distance apart. Measure the distance from the last point to the corner. Beginning at this same point on the side, trace eight evenly spaced points on the off-white portion of each side. Cut along the traced lines.

Place the wide blue strips under the side and lower edges of the quilt, adjusting them so that the raw edge of the blue is about ½″ above the top of the cut-out points. The ends of the strips will overlap. Mark where the corners of the blue strip meet one another. Remove the strips and, with right sides in, sew the corners together. Place the borders under the quilt again and pin securely. Turn in the raw edges of the quilt top and slipstitch them securely to the blue border.

Assemble the quilt layers. Quilt a feather pattern around the basket and the sham. The remainder of the quilt is quilted in diagonal lines spaced about 1″ apart.

Garland Quilt

Approximately 92″ × 107″

Fabrics

5¾ yds. off-white
3¼ yds. blue
1¼ yds. green
½ yd. light rose
⅛ yd. each light and medium lavender, dark rose and
    white
9 yds. for backing

Trace the scallop pattern, turning the tissue over to trace the second half of the scallop. Trace the garland design, placing the lower edge of the design 3¼" above the edge of the scallop.

Cut the off-white fabric in half crosswise; split one length in half lengthwise. Sew a narrow length to each side of the wider piece. Draw a line parallel to one short edge and 1" above it. Find the center of the line. Make a mark 41⅜" from the center on each side. Using a T- or L-square, draw a 90° angle at each end mark. Draw a line up each side, 97" long. Connect the lines across the top of the fabric to form a rectangle 82¾" × 97".

Placing the pattern so that the center of the scallop is at the center of the first drawn line, trace the scallop. Trace a scallop on either side of the first scallop. The scallops will meet at the top about 3¾" above the line. Repeat on the other short edge of the quilt. Find the center of the long edge. Placing the first scallop with the top point at the center, trace four scallops along each edge.

To make the corner scallop, place a yardstick between the end point of the last side scallop and the end point of the last top or bottom scallop. Mark the center point between them and note the measurement from the scallop to the point (it should be about 11½"). This measurement will be the radius of the corner scallop. Keeping the end of the yardstick at the center mark, swing it along the fabric from one scallop to the other. As you move the yardstick, mark the radius of the scallop on the fabric. Make several marks, then connect them in a smooth curve to form the corner scallop. This scallop will be considerably larger than the other scallops. Repeat on each corner.

Trace the garland pattern to the fabric, aligning the scallops exactly. The top flower of each garland is shared with the adjoining garland.

Because the corner scallop is larger than the other scallops, the garland pattern must be adjusted to fit. First, place the large flower 7" from the lower edge of the scallop and equidistant from the side and end scallops. Move the spray with the three bell flowers nearer the center of the flower. Next trace a tulip and two leaves to each side of the center flower in the same position as the ones shown on the pattern. Draw in the stem, making it conform to the shape of the scallop. Now trace a five-petaled flower on each side of the center. Draw in the two leaves, making sure that they slant toward the three-petaled flower at the top of the side or end garland.

Find the center of the quilt. Measure 20¼" both up and down from the center. Placing the center of the large flowers at these points, trace an upper and lower garland facing one another (see Fig. 1). Trace two garlands along each side of these, arranging them so that all garlands meet.

Make templates for the appliqués. Each pattern has a number indicating the color to use. Cut ⅜"-wide bias strips of green for the stems. Appliqué the stems to the quilt first. Appliqué the centers to the flowers, then appliqué the flowers and leaves to the quilt.

Cut around each scallop, 3/16" outside the drawn line.

From blue, cut two strips 9" × 84" and two strips 9" × 108" for the borders. Place these strips under the edge of the quilt to form a border. About 5" will extend past the lower edge of each scallop. Pin the strips together at the corners and mark where the corners meet. Remove the strips and, with the right sides in, sew the corners together. Place the border back under the quilt and pin securely. Turn in the edges of the scallops and blindstitch them to the border.

Assemble the quilt layers. Outline-quilt around each appliqué. Quilt the background in diagonal lines spaced 1" apart, ending the quilting ¾" from the edges of the quilt. Trim the batting and backing ½" smaller all around than the quilt top. Turn the edges of the quilt to the back and slipstitch in place.

The placement guide and appliqué patterns are on pages 24–25.

Fig. 1

Debutante's Pride Quilt

See photograph on page 7
Approximately 82″ × 104″

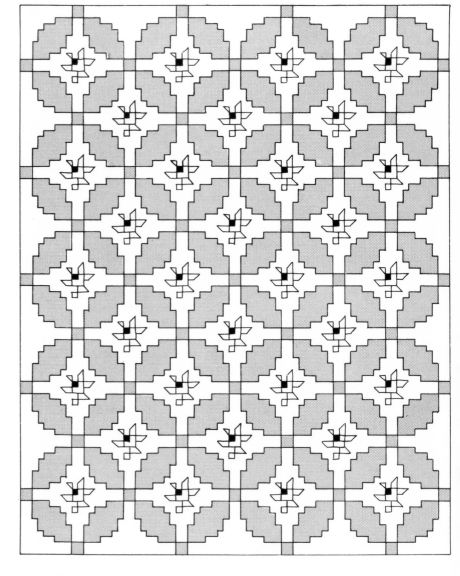

Full quilt diagram

Fabrics

8 yds. white
5¼ yds. medium blue
1 yd. light pink
½ yd. green
⅛ yd. dark pink
6 yds. for backing

Cutting across the full width of the fabric, cut 2½″-wide strips for borders—nine strips from light pink and ten strips each from white and medium blue. Join the pink strips to make two 80″ borders and two 102″ borders. Join the white strips to make two 86″ and two 108″ borders. Join the blue strips to make two 90″ and two 112″ borders. Using pattern #2 for the squares and pattern #1 for the triangles (the patterns are on page 28), cut patches following the working diagram on the inside front cover and the full quilt diagram.

Sew the green triangles and the white triangles together along the diagonal to form squares. Sew the squares together to form the center of the quilt. The completed quilt will have four full designs across and five designs down.

Sew the shorter pink borders to the top and bottom of the quilt; sew the longer borders to the sides. Sew the white, then the blue borders to the quilt in the same way.

Assemble the quilt layers. Outline-quilt around each flower. Quilt the background in diagonal lines running through the center of each blue section. Large diamonds will be formed by the quilting lines. Continue these lines onto the borders. Bind the quilt with blue.

Strawberry Quilt

Approximately 88″ × 99″

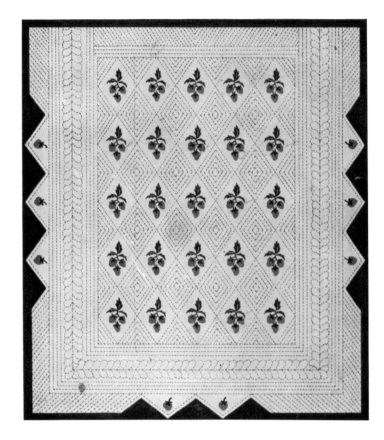

Fabrics

8 yds. off-white
3 yds. green
½ yd. red
6 yds. for backing
White six-strand embroidery floss

Trace a complete pattern for the diamond, pivoting it along the center lines. Also trace a pattern for a vertical half-diamond, a horizontal half-diamond and a quarter-diamond. Be sure to add ¼″ seam allowance to the appropriate edges of the partial diamonds. Make templates.

From off-white, cut two side panels 18″ × 100″. Cut one 18″ × 52″ and one 9″ × 52″ panel. Cut 41 whole diamonds, eight vertical half-diamonds, eight horizontal half-diamonds and four quarter-diamonds. From green, cut one strip 2″ × 88″ and six strips 2″ × 24″. Cut eleven vertical half-diamonds. Cut the appliqué pieces, cutting the berries from red and the caps, stems and leaves from green.

Trace the placement guide to the center of 25 of the whole diamonds. Appliqué the caps to the berries, then appliqué the berries to the diamonds, stuffing them lightly as you sew. With six strands of embroidery floss, work French-knot seeds as indicated by the dots on the pattern. Appliqué the leaves in place, stuffing them lightly.

Assemble the appliquéd and plain diamonds as in the photograph, filling in the edge with the half- and quarter-diamonds. Sew the pieces together in diagonal rows, then sew the rows together.

Sew the 9″-wide white strip to the top and the 18″-wide strip to the bottom. Sew on the side panels. Sew a 2″-wide green strip across the top of the quilt.

Center one of the green half-diamonds along the lower edge of the quilt, matching the raw edges. Turn in the edges and appliqué in place. Pin a green half-diamond on each side of the first. Leaving the outer edge of each half-diamond free, appliqué the inner edges in place. The side points should meet the first half-diamond about ¼″ above the edge. On each side, trim 1¾″ off the white border, starting about 1″ inside the last green half-diamond and ending at the corner. Sew a 2″-wide green strip to the white border on each side. Finish appliquéing the outer edges of the green half-diamonds, attaching them to both the white and green borders. Center four green half-diamonds along each side edge of the quilt. Trim the white border and attach the green border as before.

Appliqué a "left" strawberry to each white point along the border.

Assemble the quilt layers. Quilt around the appliqué pieces. Quilt along the center of each leaf. Follow the photograph for the remaining quilting patterns. All straight lines should be ⅛″ apart. Bind the quilt with green.

The placement guide is on page 32; the appliqué patterns are on pages 28–29.

A Quaint Pieced Quilt

Approximately 86″ × 107″

Fabrics

3¾ yds. orange
3 yds. medium yellow
2½ yds. eggshell
1¼ yds. light yellow
6¼ yds. for backing

Cutting across the full width of the fabric, cut seven 5″-wide strips of light yellow, nine 4″-wide strips of medium yellow and ten 3″-wide strips of orange. Join the strips to make one 68″ and two 98″ light yellow borders, two 78″ and two 106″ medium yellow borders and two 90″ and two 110″ orange borders. Cut seventeen 13½″ squares from orange. Using pattern #2 on page 28 and the working diagram below, cut patches for eighteen blocks.

Sew the patches together to form 13½″ squares. Sew the pieced squares and the large orange squares together in seven rows of five, alternating the squares. The first, third, fifth and seventh rows will begin with a pieced square; the second, fourth and sixth rows will begin with an orange square.

Sew the light yellow borders to the lower edge, then to the sides of the quilt. Sew the medium yellow borders to the top and bottom, then to the sides. Sew on the orange borders in the same way.

Assemble the quilt layers. The plain blocks can be quilted with any large quilting motif. The pieced blocks and the unquilted portions of the plain blocks should be quilted in diagonal rows 1¼″ apart. On the first horizontal row of blocks, these lines should run from the lower right to the upper left. On the next row, the lines should run from lower left to upper right. Alternate these two rows. The light yellow border can be quilted with any border quilting design. Continue the zigzag pattern of diagonal lines on the two outer borders. Bind the quilt with orange.

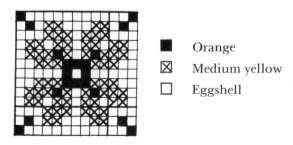

■ Orange
⊠ Medium yellow
□ Eggshell

Jonquil Quilt placement guide

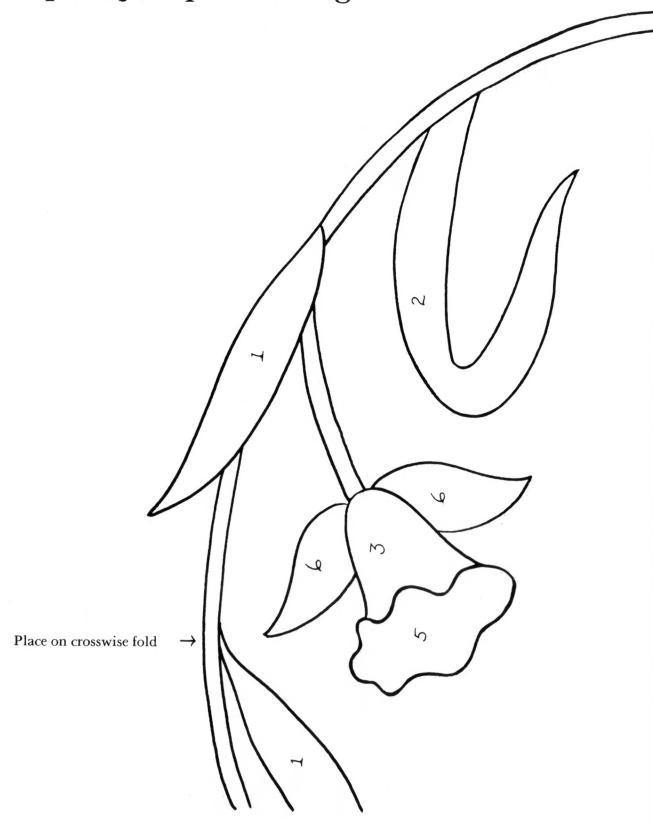

Place on crosswise fold →

Place on lengthwise fold

Place on crosswise fold

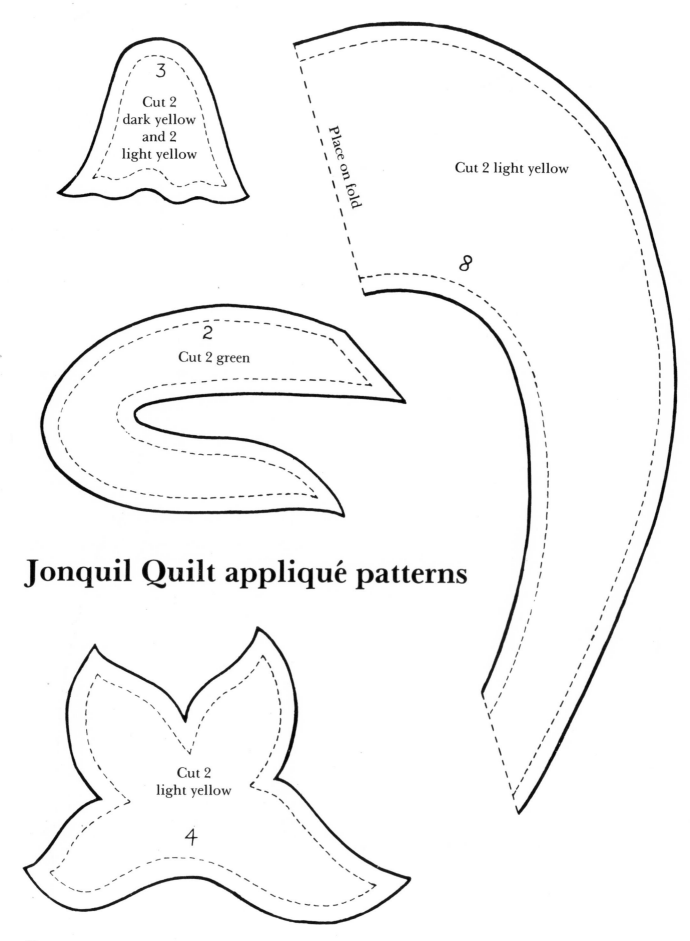

3

Cut 2
dark yellow
and 2
light yellow

Place on fold

Cut 2 light yellow

8

2

Cut 2 green

Jonquil Quilt appliqué patterns

Cut 2
light yellow

4

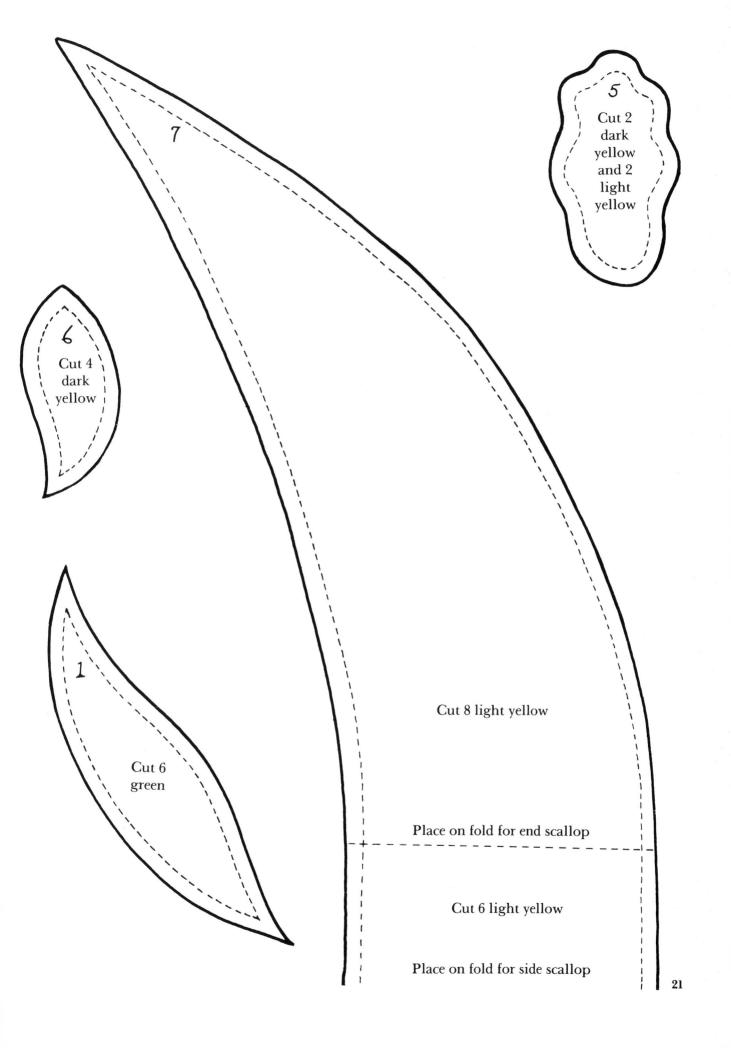

7

5

Cut 2
dark
yellow
and 2
light
yellow

6

Cut 4
dark
yellow

1

Cut 6
green

Cut 8 light yellow

Place on fold for end scallop

Cut 6 light yellow

Place on fold for side scallop

21

Garland Quilt placement guide and appliqué patterns

Place tip of leaf
3¼″ up from scallop

Scallop half

Place on

1. Blue
2. Light rose
3. Dark rose
4. Light lavender
5. Medium lavender
6. White
7. Green

Same
flower
as on
opposite
side

Patchwork patterns

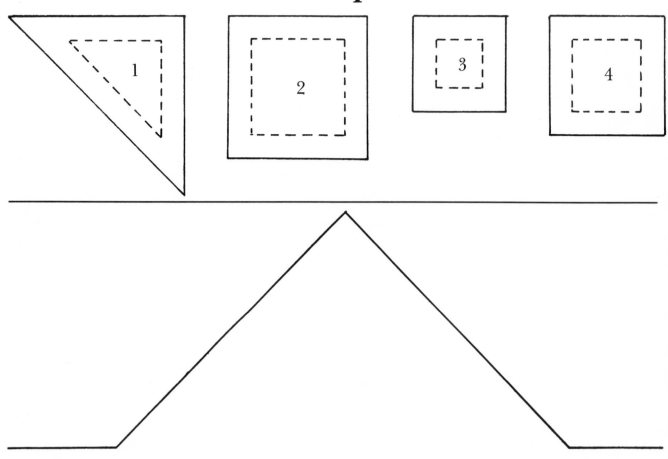

Heirloom Basket Quilt point cutting guide

Strawberry Quilt

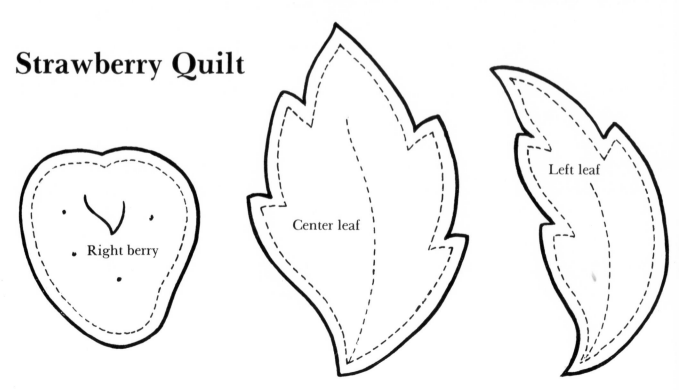

Right berry

Center leaf

Left leaf

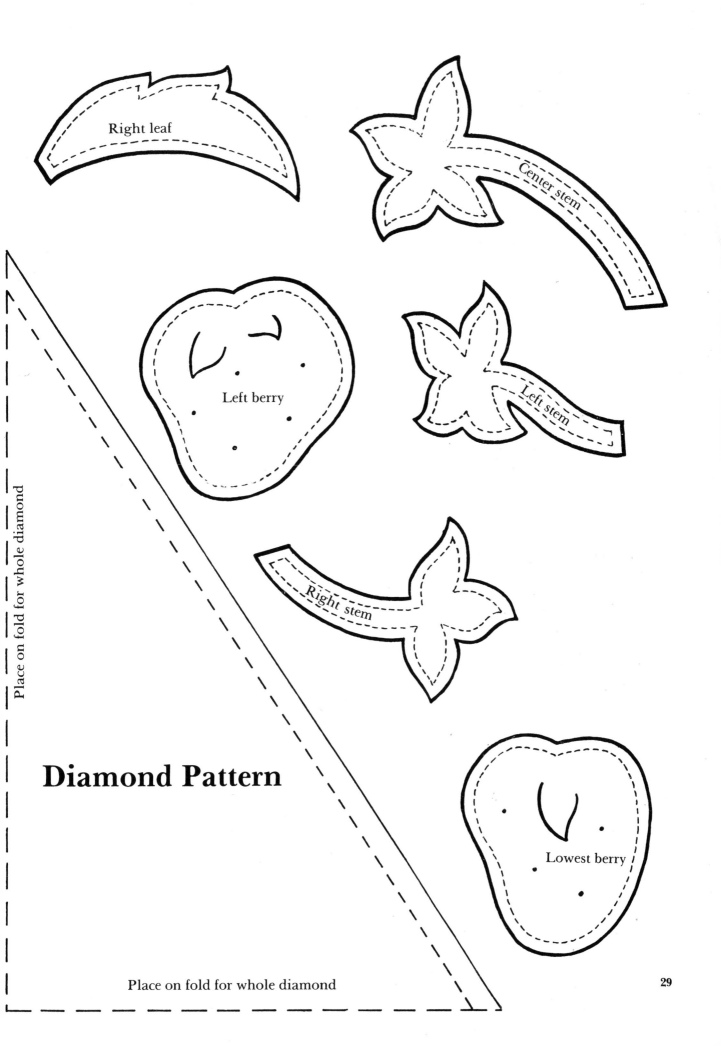

Right leaf

Center stem

Left berry

Left stem

Right stem

Diamond Pattern

Lowest berry

Strawberry Quilt

placement guide